Mother Goose

JAZZ CHANTS ®

CAROLYN GRAHAM

Illustrations by:

Yvette Banek
Sandy Forrest
Daniele Imperiale
Kathleen McCord
Lane Yerkes

Oxford University Press

To Saori Ogose-Someya

Table of Contents

RHYMES

♪ SONGS

Structure Key

* denotes that all variations to the rhyme or song practice the structure.

WHAT IS *MOTHER GOOSE JAZZ CHANTS*®?

Mother Goose Jazz Chants® is a collection of 28 traditional rhymes and songs, each followed by one or more variations. The original rhymes and songs allow students of English to share in the oral tradition common to many who live in English-speaking countries. The variations provide further practice with the rhythm, stress, and intonation patterns of English.

GENERAL NOTES

General suggestions for presenting the rhymes and songs are listed below. Note that these are only suggestions. You should feel free to experiment and improvise to meet the needs of your own students.

Presenting the Rhymes

Step 1   Read the rhyme at natural speed. Students listen.

Step 2   Explain any unfamiliar words. Point out rhyming words and have students repeat them.

Step 3   Read the rhyme line by line. Students repeat after each line.

Step 4   Play the cassette. Students listen.

Step 5   Ask questions about the characters in the rhyme. For example, questions about "Mary had a little lamb" could include: *What kind of pet did Mary have? Was he big? Did he follow her to school? Where did he go every day?*

Presenting the Songs

Step 1   Play the cassette. Students listen.

Step 2   Explain any unfamiliar words. Point out rhyming words and have students repeat them.

Step 3   Read the lyrics line by line. Students repeat after each line.

Step 4   Sing the song (melody only) line by line. Students repeat after each line. To teach the melody without the lyrics, use "da da da" instead of the words.

Step 5   Play the cassette. Students sing along.

Extension Activities

There are many possible extension activities you can do to reinforce the new language. A few examples follow:

• Retell one of the rhymes, changing key information as you go along. For example, change "There was an old woman who lived in a shoe" to "There was a young man who lived in a shoe". Students stop you whenever they hear a change, and provide the correct word or words.

• Sing part of one of the songs, then stop. Students must sing the missing word or words. For example, sing "Are you…". Students must sing "sleeping".

• Write a rhyme or a song on a piece of paper. Cut the paper into strips, with only one line on each strip. Scramble the strips, and have students put them back in order. For added challenge, include more than one rhyme or song in the pile of strips.

• Several of the rhymes and songs have actions that are traditionally associated with the lyrics, including "This little piggy went to market", "Twinkle, twinkle, little star", and "The itsy bitsy spider". Teach actions along with the lyrics whenever possible, since associating actions with words is a great aid to memorization.

• There are many rhymes and songs which lend themselves well to role-playing. Role-playing helps to contextualize the vocabulary for the students. To do a role-play, assign roles to selected students, and have them act out what is happening in the rhyme or song. For example, if doing "Mary had a little lamb", assign one student as Mary, one as the lamb, and several students as the children at school. The students act out the story while the rest of the class says the rhyme.

• Encourage students to share rhymes and songs from their own cultures with the rest of the class.

Mary had a little lamb,

His fleece was white as snow;

And everywhere that Mary went

The lamb was sure to go.

He followed her to school one day,

Which was against the rule;

It made the children laugh and play

To see a lamb at school.

Danny had a little dog,
Her name was Mary Lou;
Whenever Danny took a nap
His dog got sleepy, too.

Harry had a little horse,
Her name was Baby Mary;
Whenever Baby went to town
She always carried Harry.

Betty had a talking bird,
His name was Little Joe;
Whenever Betty said, "Good-bye"
The bird said, "Hi, hello."

Good-bye!

Hi, hello!

Jack be nimble,
Jack be quick,
Jack jump over
The candlestick.

Jack be friendly,
Don't be shy,
Don't forget
To say good-bye.

Get up, Jackie,
Don't be late!
Our English class
Begins at eight.

Jack be careful!
Do your best!
Don't forget
You have a test!

There was an old woman who lived in a shoe,

She had so many children she didn't know what to do;

She gave them some broth without any bread,

Then gave them a spanking and put them to bed.

There was an old woman who lived in a sock

With a clock that went "tick" and a clock that went "tock";

One day she got angry and threw a big rock

At the clock that went "tick" and the clock that went "tock."

There was an old woman who lived in a hat.

Her nights were so lonely she bought a big cat.

The cat got so hungry he ate all her rice,

He ate all her popcorn, he ate all her mice.

7

Fuzzy Wuzzy was a bear.

Fuzzy Wuzzy had no hair.

Fuzzy Wuzzy wasn't very fuzzy,

Was he?

Busy Lizzie is a bee.

Lizzie works from one to three.

Busy Lizzie isn't very busy,

Is she?

Little Willy was a flea.

Willy drank a pot of tea.

Little Willy won't be very chilly,

Will he?

Itty Bitty was a dog.

Itty Bitty hated smog.

Itty Bitty didn't like the city,

Did he?

9

Hickory, dickory, dock

Hickory, dickory, dock,

The mouse ran up the clock.

The clock struck one,

The mouse ran down,

Hickory, dickory, dock.

Hickory, dickory, hock,

I think I lost my sock.

I had it on,

But now it's gone,

Hickory, dickory, hock.

Huckery, duckery, hick,

I found a baby chick.

The chick said, "Peep"

And fell asleep,

Huckery, duckery, hick.

Hickory, dickory, duck,

I named my chipmunk Chuck.

I wanted to play,

But he ran away,

Hickory, dickory, duck.

Ladybird, ladybird

Ladybird, ladybird,

Fly away home.

Your house is on fire,

Your children will burn;

All except one,

And her name is Anne.

She crept under

The frying pan.

Rocking horse, rocking horse,

Don't run away.

The children are coming,

They all want to play.

Rocking horse, rocking horse,

Don't try to hide.

The children are coming,

They all want a ride.

Papa bear, Papa bear,

Run along home.

Your children are crying,

They're home all alone.

Take them some apples.

Take them some pears.

Take them some candy.

They're good little bears.

Teddy Bear, Teddy Bear, turn around

Teddy Bear, Teddy Bear, turn around.

Teddy Bear, Teddy Bear, touch the ground.

Teddy Bear, Teddy Bear, shut the door.

Teddy Bear, Teddy Bear, count to four.

Teddy Bear, Teddy Bear, turn out the light.

Teddy Bear, Teddy Bear, say goodnight.

Baby Bear, Baby Bear, touch your knees.

Baby Bear, Baby Bear, please say please.

Baby Bear, Baby Bear, blow your nose.

Baby Bear, Baby Bear, wash your clothes.

Baby Bear, Baby Bear, please don't cry.

Baby Bear, Baby Bear, say good-bye.

Granny Bear, Granny Bear, please sit down.

Granny Bear, Granny Bear, please don't frown.

Granny Bear, Granny Bear, let's make tea.

Granny Bear, Granny Bear, stay with me.

Granny Bear, Granny Bear, don't say no.

Granny Bear, Granny Bear, please don't go.

15

This little piggy went to market,

This little piggy stayed home,

This little piggy had roast beef,

This little piggy had none,

And this little piggy cried, "Wee, wee, wee,"

All the way home.

This little chicken is silly,
This little chicken is smart,
This little chicken likes music,
This little chicken loves art,
And this little chicken said,
  "Wow! Wow! Wow!"
All the way home.

This little bird's taking lessons,
This little bird can't fly,
This little bird is lazy,
This little bird won't try,
And this little bird cried,
  "Oh no! Not me! Oh no!"
All the way home.

Diddle, diddle, dumpling, my son John,

Went to bed with his trousers on;

One shoe off, and one shoe on,

Diddle, diddle, dumpling, my son John.

18

Doodle, doodle, doughnuts, my dog Don,

Took a bath with his raincoat on;

One sock off, and one sock on,

Doodle, doodle, doughnuts, my dog Don.

Fiddle, faddle, fruitcake, my friend Fran,

Goes to sleep in a frying pan;

Sleeps all morning, if she can,

Fiddle, faddle, fruitcake, my friend Fran.

Chiddle, diddle, cheesecake, my friend Fred,

Went to sea in a double bed;

Two soft pillows for his head,

Chiddle, diddle, cheesecake, my friend Fred.

Humpty Dumpty sat on a wall

Humpty Dumpty sat on a wall;

Humpty Dumpty had a big fall.

All the king's horses and all the king's men

Couldn't put Humpty together again.

Bumpty Wumpty ran in the house;

Bumpty Wumpty tripped on a mouse.

All the Queens' husbands and all the Kings' wives

Laughed about Bumpty the rest of their lives.

Fussy Gussy went to a dance;

Fussy Gussy wore his new pants.

Stripes on his necktie, stripes on his suit,

Fussy Gussy looked very cute.

Little Jack Horner sat in a corner,

Eating his Christmas pie;

He stuck in his thumb, and pulled out a plum,

And said, "What a good boy am I!"

Little Miss Muffet sat on a tuffet,

Eating her curds and whey;

Along came a spider, who sat down beside her,

And frightened Miss Muffet away.

Little Miss Myrtle sat on a turtle,

Thinking that it was a chair;

"Oww eee!," cried the turtle,

"I'm sorry," said Myrtle,

"I didn't know you were there."

Little Amanda sat on a panda,

Eating an ice-cream cone;

The panda said, "Ouch! I'm a bear, not a couch.

Go away, please leave me alone."

Jack and Jill went up the hill,

To fetch a pail of water;

Jack fell down and broke his crown,

And Jill came tumbling after.

Jack and Jane jumped on a plane,

To fly to Barcelona;

What a surprise!

They rubbed their eyes,

And saw their sister Mona!

Kate and Pete ran down the street,

To catch the bus for Dallas;

"Oh," said Kate, "I know we're late,

But we have to wait for Alice."

Georgie Porgie, pudding and pie

Georgie Porgie, pudding and pie,

Kissed the girls and made them cry;

When the boys came out to play,

Georgie Porgie ran away.

Franky Panky, pepper and cheese,

Kissed the girls and made them sneeze;

When they said, "Achoo! Achoo!"

Franky started sneezing, too.

Polly Wolly, sugar and cream,

Kissed the boys and made them scream;

When the girls came out to play,

Polly Wolly ran away.

There was a little girl who had a little curl
Right in the middle of her forehead;
When she was good, she was very, very good,
But when she was bad, she was horrid.

28

There was a little mouse who built a little house

Right in the middle of the highway;

When friends said, "No, you can't stay there,"

He said, "I'll do it my way."

There was a little goat who sailed a little boat

Right down the middle of the river;

When it was hot, he was very, very hot,

And when it was cold, he would shiver.

Twinkle, twinkle, little star,

How I wonder what you are!

Up above the world so high,

Like a diamond in the sky.

Twinkle, twinkle, little star,

How I wonder what you are!

Raindrops falling all around,

Falling, falling, on the ground.

On the mountains, on the seas,

Falling on the Christmas trees.

Raindrops falling all around,

Falling, falling, on the ground.

Snowflakes falling all around,

Falling, falling, on the ground.

Falling here and falling there,

On my nose and on my hair.

Snowflakes falling all around,

Falling, falling, on the ground.

Here we go 'round the mulberry bush

Here we go 'round the mulberry bush,
The mulberry bush, the mulberry bush.
Here we go 'round the mulberry bush,
So early in the morning.

This is the way we wash our clothes,
Wash our clothes, wash our clothes.
This is the way we wash our clothes,
So early in the morning.

I'm going to take my dog to school,
Dog to school, dog to school.
He's going to learn a grammar rule,
Early Monday morning.

He's going to learn to count to three,
Count to three, count to three.
He's going to learn the verb "to be,"
Early Monday morning.

London Bridge is falling down

London Bridge is falling down,
Falling down, falling down.
London Bridge is falling down,
My fair lady.

Build it up with sticks and stones,
Sticks and stones, sticks and stones.
Build it up with sticks and stones,
My fair lady.

Mary Brown was born today,
Born today, born today.
Mary's ten years old today.
Happy birthday!

We know who was born today,
Born today, born today.
We know you were born today.
Happy birthday!

Happy birthday, Mary Brown,
Mary Brown, Mary Brown.
Happy birthday, Mary Brown,
Happy birthday!

Rock-a-bye, baby, on the treetop,

When the wind blows the cradle will rock;

When the bough breaks the cradle will fall,

And down will come baby, cradle, and all.

Here are the questions on the exam,

Please read the questions as fast as you can;

Answer the questions, don't be too slow.

When you are finished, then you can go.

I know the answers, I know them well,

I know the answers, but I won't tell;

I know the answers, I know them well,

I know all the answers, but I won't tell.

Are you sleeping?

Are you sleeping?

Are you sleeping?

Brother John, Brother John?

Morning bells are ringing

Morning bells are ringing

Ding, ding, dong,

Ding, ding, dong.

That's my mother,

That's my brother,

That's my dad,

That's my dad.

That's my little sister,

That's my baby sister,

She looks mad.

She looks mad.

That's my teacher,

That's my teacher,

Mrs. Green,

Mrs. Green.

That's my Uncle Jimmy,

That's my cousin Timmy,

That's Aunt Jean,

She's sixteen.

The farmer in the dell

The farmer in the dell,
The farmer in the dell,
Heigh ho, the derry-o,
The farmer in the dell.

The farmer takes a wife,
The farmer takes a wife,
Heigh ho, the derry-o,
The farmer takes a wife.

Additional verses:

The wife takes a child

The child takes a nurse

The nurse takes a dog

The dog takes a cat

The cat takes a rat

The rat takes the cheese

The cheese stands alone

It's time to go to school,

It's time to go to school,

Look! Now it's eight o'clock,

It's time to go to school.

It's time to have your lunch,

It's time to have your lunch,

Look! Now it's twelve o'clock,

It's time to have your lunch.

It's time to go to bed,

It's time to go to bed,

Look! Now it's ten o'clock,

It's time to go to bed.

Old MacDonald had a farm, E I E I O.

And on that farm he had some sheep, E I E I O.

With a baa baa here, and a baa baa there,

Here a baa, there a baa, everywhere a baa baa.

Old MacDonald had a farm, E I E I O.

Additional verses:

cows (moo moo)

pigs (oink oink)

chickens (cluck cluck)

He eats chicken soup for lunch
Every day at noon.
He eats chicken soup for lunch
Every day at noon.
Chicken soup, chicken soup,
Monday, Tuesday, Wednesday, Thursday
Chicken soup, chicken soup,
Friday, Saturday, twice on Sunday.
He eats chicken soup for lunch
Every day at noon.

43

Oh dear, what can the matter be?

Oh dear, what can the matter be?

Dear, dear, what can the matter be?

Oh dear, what can the matter be?

Johnny's so long at the fair.

He promised to buy me a bunch of blue ribbons,

He promised to buy me a bunch of blue ribbons,

He promised to buy me a bunch of blue ribbons,

To tie up my bonny brown hair.

She loves noodles for breakfast,

And he loves kimchi for breakfast,

And they love cornflakes for breakfast,

But I love bananas and cream.

She loves strawberry ice cream,

And he loves chocolate chip ice cream,

And they love peppermint ice cream,

But I love bananas and cream.

45

Oh where, oh where has my little dog gone?

Oh where, oh where can he be?

With his ears cut short and his tail cut long,

Oh where, oh where can he be?

46

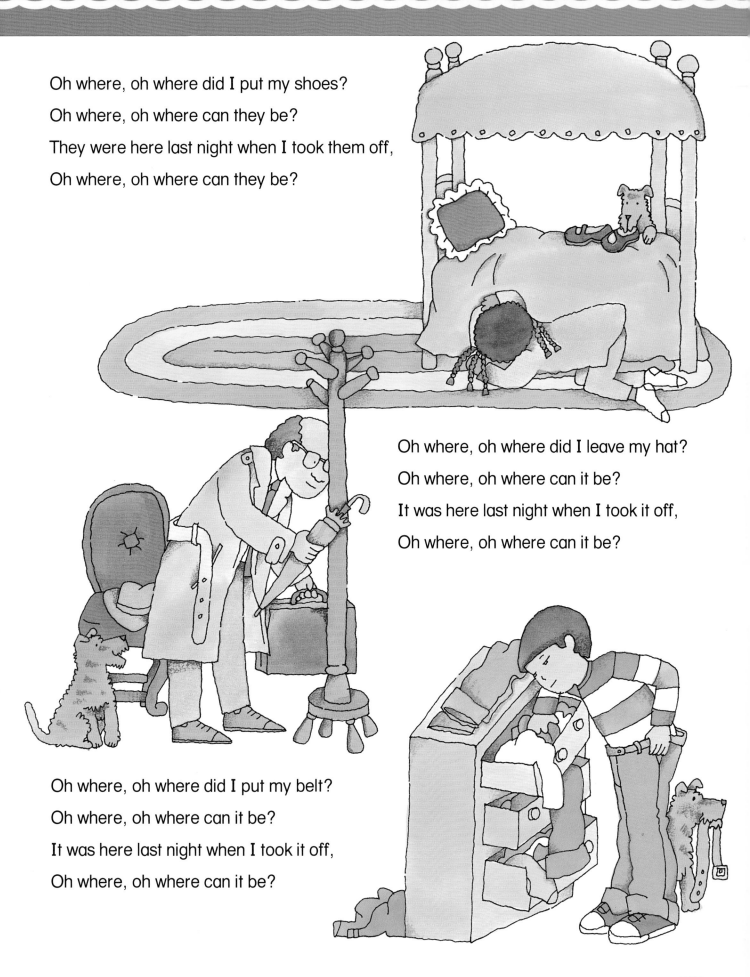

Oh where, oh where did I put my shoes?
Oh where, oh where can they be?
They were here last night when I took them off,
Oh where, oh where can they be?

Oh where, oh where did I leave my hat?
Oh where, oh where can it be?
It was here last night when I took it off,
Oh where, oh where can it be?

Oh where, oh where did I put my belt?
Oh where, oh where can it be?
It was here last night when I took it off,
Oh where, oh where can it be?

Three blind mice,

Three blind mice,

See how they run!

See how they run!

They all ran after the farmer's wife,

Who cut off their tails with a carving knife;

Have you ever seen such a sight in your life,

As three blind mice?

48

Three fat cats,

Three fat cats,

Chasing rats.

Chasing rats.

Papa cat's running all over the floor,

Mama cat's trying to catch three or four,

Baby cat's hiding behind the front door,

Three fat cats.

Lazy Mary, will you get up?

Will you get up?

Will you get up?

Lazy Mary, will you get up?

So early in the morning.

50

Lazy Larry, will you wake up?

Will you wake up?

Will you wake up?

Lazy Larry, will you wake up?

Don't fall asleep in the classroom.

Noisy Nelly, will you sit down?

Will you sit down?

Will you sit down?

Noisy Nelly, will you sit down?

Don't run around in the classroom.

Silly Billy, will you be good?

Will you be good?

Will you be good?

Silly Billy, will you be good?

Don't fool around in the classroom.

Row, row, row your boat

Row, row, row your boat,

Gently down the stream.

Merrily, merrily, merrily, merrily,

Life is but a dream.

Learn, learn, learn the words,
Every word I say.
Practice reading, writing, speaking
English every day.

Write, write, write the words,
Try to spell them right.
Practice reading, writing, speaking
English every night.

Read, read, read the words,
Study what I say.
Practice reading, writing, speaking
English every day.

Have you ever seen a lassie, a lassie, a lassie? 〜〜

Have you ever seen a lassie, a lassie, a lassie?

Have you ever seen a lassie go this way and that?

Go this way and that way

And this way and that way.

Have you ever seen a lassie go this way and that?

54

Have you ever seen a panda, a panda, a panda?

    No, I've never seen a panda.

Well, neither have I.

    But I've seen a monkey.

    And I've seen a lion.

Well, I've seen a zebra.

And I've seen a tiger,

But I've never seen a panda.

    Well, neither have I.

The itsy bitsy spider

The itsy bitsy spider
Went up the water spout.
Down came the rain
And washed the spider out.
Out came the sun
And dried up all the rain,
And the itsy bitsy spider
Went up the spout again.

Little baby blackbird
Sitting in a tree.
Little baby blackbird
Waiting patiently.
Down flew a bad bird
Who pushed him all around,
And the little baby blackbird
Fell down on the ground.

Little baby blackbird
Started to cry.
Little baby blackbird
Hadn't learned to fly.
"Oh," said a nice bird.
"You can follow me."
And the little baby blackbird
Flew back to the tree.